Investing

An Instructional Guide On Commencing Investment In
Short Term Rentals, Maximizing Returns From Initial
Properties, And Establishing A Framework For
Supplementing Monthly Earnings Presently

Henry Robinson

TABLE OF CONTENT

Earning Of Passive Income Through Dividend Stocks

Passive income pertains to the funds one consistently acquires with minimal exertion or involvement. This stipulation is applicable in cases where one continues to receive regular financial compensation on a daily, monthly, quarterly, or annual basis, while refraining from active involvement in the operational aspects of the underlying investment. Not every investment will yield passive income. A widely favored investment opportunity that has the potential to generate a substantial income is dividend stock.

Companies always pay dividends. When a company generates a surplus, it may opt to distribute a portion of these earnings to its shareholders through dividend disbursements. Many corporations adopt this practice on a quarterly basis, or in accordance with a predetermined payment schedule. Some individuals or institutions disburse the payments annually, biannually, or even triannually.

Investing your financial resources into a corporation that distributes regular dividends presents itself as one of the most effective methods to generate passive revenue. The income one receives from dividend stocks is contingent upon both the capital alloc

An instance that illustrates this phenomenon is observed in the S&P international dividend exchange-traded fund (ETF), wherein a dividend payment of 5.4% is disbursed to its shareholders on an annual basis. This implies that a principal investment of $100,000 in this company would yield an annual dividend of $5,400. Due to the company's payment structure, a sum of $1350 will be disbursed to you once every four months.

A notable benefit of utilizing dividend stocks for passive income generation lies in the fact that it exempts you from the obligation of actively managing your investment portfolio. However, a downside exists in the form of companies being vested with the obligation to ascertain the annual amount you are eligible to receive. This implies that selecting a company that offers comparatively low percentages will result in receiving meager dividends annually. The act of engaging in the investment of dividend stocks necessitates the allocation of a certain amount of time and diligent oversight of one's stock portfolio. Numerous applications have been developed that facilitate accomplishing this task irrespective of your geographical location. In order for passive income to be achieved, it is crucial to make investments in a significant quantity of shares. As the number of shares increases, so does the income.

Dividend Stocks

Equities that are associated with dividends exhibit superior potential for generating passive income. After the acquisition of such securities, your dividends will accumulate progressively as you consistently make further investments. Dividends, in their essence, denote remunerations accorded to shareholders of a particular enterprise in correlation to the company's profitability. You have the option to either reinvest your dividends into additional shares or receive them as cash disbursements. Given that dividend amounts differ between companies, it is imperative to ascertain the optimal investment choice that will enable one to achieve maximum returns. If you possess uncertainties regarding appropriate stocks for investment, it is advisable to adhere to those endowed with the prestigious designation of 'dividend aristocrat'. Typically, these stocks are characterized by a consistent track record of generating substantial dividend payouts throughout the past 25 years.

One illustration of this is observed when Company B offers its shares at a valuation of $100 per share. The stipulated amount of dividends associated with each share is approximately $5. To acquire the yearly dividend yield, one must calculate the product of the dividend percentage and the total quantity of shares. In the event that you have made an investment of, for instance, 100 shares in the company, your collective dividends will amount to 5 multiplied by 100, thereby yielding a sum of $500 annually as passive income.

This elucidates the reason behind the perennially elevated demand for dividend stocks. In addition to bestowing upon you a form of passive income, dividends also serve as a safeguard against potential losses. In the event that a portion of your investment is lost, dividends will assist in mitigating this loss. Should the stock prices maintain a state of stagnation, resulting in no realization of profit, you will nonetheless receive some income through the disbursement of dividends. When engaging in the investment of dividend stocks, it is imperative to exercise caution in regards to dividend yields that display an exceptionally high deviation from the norm. These symptoms consistently point to underlying issues or problems within the company being discussed. Typically, a dividend yield ranging from 3 to 6 percent would be deemed conventional in nature.

Investment Strategies

In the forthcoming chapter, we will thoroughly examine the primary investment strategies employed by long-term investors. The category of investors who employ a buy-and-hold strategy encompasses those who specifically focus on dividend investments. A variety of methods are employed, with the primary approach being to refrain from allocating excessive resources into a sole stock or a limited number of stocks, thereby mitigating the risk of potential losses stemming from a negative outcome in said investment. Moreover, it is advisable to refrain from making purchases during unfavorable moments. While traders may attempt to impress with their signals and tactics, discerning the precise points at which the market attains its peak or trough, or predicting the reversal of trends, is essentially unachievable. In the span of a considerable duration, purchasing even at the highest price points can yield substantial profits; nonetheless, we shall present a methodology that will assist you in circumventing such imprudent decisions. Furthermore, we will be discussing the potential need for portfolio rebalancing in your specific situation, in addition to determining the appropriate timing for divesting from a particular stock.

Various Forms of Risk Encountered by Investors

As an investor, you will encounter various categories of risk. As an illustration, let's consider a scenario where an individual decides to make an investment in a company that becomes entangled in a high-profile controversy, subsequently resulting in a significant decline of its share value to a level comparable to that of penny stocks. Alternatively, you may find yourself heavily committed when a substantial economic downturn occurs, resulting in a significant decline in the value of nearly every stock as investors frantically seek to divest their holdings.

Additionally, there exist various other potential risks. There exist risks associated with the holistic performance of the economy, risks linked to fluctuating inflation rates, and risks associated with fluctuating interest rates.

Certain risks are intrinsically linked to the stock market, whereas there are additional risks that do not bear such a connection. Certain individuals wield significant influence over the stock market, despite not being directly involved in it.

When a risk factor extends beyond the confines of the stock market, such as GDP growth or the inflation rate, and has a pervasive impact on every individual stock, it is referred to as systemic risk. These forms of risk are not confined to a specific sector or individual stock, and such risks are predominantly beyond the purview of individuals.

Non-systemic risks pertain exclusively to an individual company, industry, or sector. Therefore, this could entail a challenge affecting the financial industry, or perhaps an issue affecting the technology sector. Occasionally, there may arise risks that solely affect a singular stock or a small subset, while leaving others unaffected. As an illustration, one might observe a scenario wherein Netflix experiences a decline, whereas Facebook and Google demonstrate an upward trajectory. Perhaps Netflix experienced a decline in subscription numbers, leading to a potential disruption of their services. This could potentially have a significant effect on the stock value of Netflix; however, it will not exert any influence on other companies. If anything, in the event that it did have an influence on other companies, one would envision that it might even prove advantageous to them, particularly if they provide any sort of similar service. As an illustration, Apple offers a product known as Apple

TV, whereas Amazon provides a service called Amazon Prime. These services could potentially derive advantages from individuals shifting away from Netflix, thus resulting in an upward trajectory of the share prices of these companies amidst a notable decline in the share price of Netflix.

The primary means through which one can mitigate exposure to systemic risk is by employing the strategy of dollar cost averaging. That, in fact, does not precisely align with the primary objective of dollar cost averaging; however, it is a strategy that effectively mitigates the impact of market downturns on your investment portfolio. It is crucial to note that the utilization of dollar cost averaging, along with a consistent expenditure at fixed intervals, enables an effective approach for mitigating the type of systemic risk under discussion through strategic acquisition of shares during market downturns.

Diversification is employed as a means of addressing non-systemic risk. If you diversify your portfolio, you will experience reduced vulnerability to fluctuations in a few individual companies, thereby mitigating the impact of market volatility.

Investors frequently employ diversification as a measure to mitigate systemic risk, by allocating their funds across various investment classes. Thus, they will allocate a portion of funds to be held in cash, allocate another portion to be invested in government bonds, and allocate a final portion to be invested in corporate bonds. While it is feasible to engage in such activities while simultaneously adhering to a dividend investment strategy, it is crucial to note that this book primarily emphasizes different subject matter. If you have a genuine inclination to invest your funds in cash or bonds, we kindly suggest seeking a reliable source to provide you with suitable guidance throughout this endeavor.

Society holds hard work in high esteem and commends those who embody it. A retired individual will typically provide information about their past work experience, even in the absence of an inquiry. When individuals who are unattached come across each other and embark on a social outing, occupations frequently serve as one of the initial subjects to initiate the discourse. In this literary work, I commence with an introductory depiction of my initial employment endeavor as a dishwasher in a nightclub, thereby acquainting the reader with my personal background.

A significant number of individuals find it more convenient to establish a connection with an individual of industrious disposition and effectiveness, as opposed to an individual who lacks diligence. When analyzing the notion of "labor", it is readily comprehensible to conceive the idea of the agreement between the employee and employer, wherein the employee dedicates ample hours, considerable energy, and comparable effort to the employer, while the employer oversees the employee in return with the assurance of remuneration and, at times, the supplementary advantage of fostering a sense of affiliation.

The global community requires individuals who demonstrate diligence and dedication in their endeavors. They are essential for the development of any advancing society. Nonetheless, the aforementioned culture that prioritizes career above all else can also have adverse effects and create a toxic environment. One can dedicate oneself to diligent efforts over the course of a lifetime and strategically prepare for a pleasurable retirement. During the initial phase of your life, one tends to jeopardize their well-being in pursuit of financial gains, while in the latter stage, financial resources are allocated towards enhancing one's health. Such is the prevailing norm in present times, with this being more commonly observed rather than being an isolated occurrence. You allocate a considerable amount of time to your professional responsibilities, yet allocate a disproportionately small amount of time to hobbies, personal growth, and, regrettably, your loved ones. I aim to divulge the clandestine strategy for disrupting this detrimental pattern at this very moment -

through the accumulation of assets that generate income.

Employment is crucial for both financial security and maintaining good mental well-being. The fundamental human desire to contribute and experience a sense of usefulness is inherent throughout history. Therefore, this book does not advocate for resigning from your current employment. You shall also not receive any expedited methods for accumulating wealth. However, employing this method of minimal effort will assist in gradually transitioning away from your detrimental work schedule. This strategic approach eliminates the element of fate, demonstrating the feasibility of achieving financial independence well in advance of the anticipated retirement age. Gradually over the course of time, you will be able to transform the countless hours spent commuting to work, trivial conversations around the watercooler, unproductive meetings, and mundane projects into a life imbued with significance and direction.

This literature offers a methodical and convenient approach to amassing appreciating assets over time, thereby granting the desired goal of financial independence. Through persistent effort, self-control, and the virtue of being patient, you will gradually observe the transition of your current employment from being the sole provider of income to merely one among various sources – ultimately, it might even reach a point where you decide to relinquish it as a source of income altogether.

Presently, the contemporary open market has bestowed upon humanity numerous exceptional benefits, among which the most pivotal is the liberty to deliberate between an actively engaged occupation, a passive investment scheme, or a fusion of the two. An unfortunate aspect of this situation is the presence of systematic structural impediments that hinder individuals with limited savings from accessing the full range of free-market opportunities that are at their disposal. Those individuals also make valuable contributions to the development of the economy, yet the economy fails to reciprocate any benefits towards them.

It is an incontrovertible fact that in a democratic nation like our own, individuals have the rightful opportunity to establish an investment account, thus commencing the process of acquiring a stake in productive assets. Nevertheless, the plight faced by diligent and committed employees lies in the fact that due to the limited duration of twenty-four hours per day, the majority find themselves encountering significant challenges when it comes to contemplating the prospect of partaking in a retirement lifestyle, let alone having the financial means to support it.

With the aid of this literary piece, my intention is to not only provide you with that alternative, but also extend further possibilities.

Investment & Time

While the majority of individuals employed in the labor force actively deliberate on placing their funds within the capital market, they frequently decline the notion and concurrently express an abundance of justifications.

I am currently pressed for time." "I am unable to allocate any time at the moment."

I have been informed that there is a possibility of a

significant decline in the stock market."

I am completely unaware of what my current actions or decisions should be.

Are any of these recognizable to you? I endorse the notion of allowing yourself ample time to peruse through the pages of this concise literary work. I desire for you to acquire a comprehensive comprehension of the process, thereby fostering an augmentation of your self-assurance in the allocation of your financial resources. There is a brief time period separating the moment you choose to be the esteemed proprietor of an investment portfolio and the moment that you officially assume ownership.

Possessing a passive investment portfolio will grant you legitimate ownership stakes in numerous companies, thereby affording you the privileges associated with ownership. As the passage of time ensues, you will gradually discern the pronounced correlation between company profits and the growth exhibited in your investment portfolio, thereby witnessing the exponential appreciation of your capital assets.

However, it is premature at this stage to delve into specifics regarding numerical data. I kindly request your patience.

The objective of money is to provide contentment and assurance to its possessor. Throughout the course of time, a well-managed stock

investment portfolio has
the potential to generate
substantial financial
gains. Upon conducting a
comprehensive analysis
of your financial records
at the conclusion of the
fiscal year, you may
promptly discover that
your primary occupation
solely constitutes a mere
fraction of the total
earnings amassed
throughout the preceding
twelve-month period.

Certainly, you have the unrestricted freedom to discontinue your participation in the market by divesting your ownership interests at any point in time. After a significant investment period of five or ten years, one has the option to divest all assets and acquire something new and visually appealing. I would advise retaining your investment in the financial markets, although ultimately the decision lies in your discretion. Nevertheless, it is my belief that you may have a preference for perpetuating your investments, with the ultimate goal of achieving financial independence, enabling you to autonomously determine when it is suitable to depart from your current occupation and potentially experience an enhanced quality of life.

The inert investment approach outlined in this publication is characterized by its simplicity, reliability, and unwavering nature. As an investor inclined towards a more cautious approach, it is prudent for you to anticipate a gradual pace of growth during the initial phases.

However, you can have confidence in the substantial influence and support provided by compound interest. Although it might appear inconceivable and implausible at present, in the upcoming chapter of this literature, you shall be introduced to Thomas, an enterprising distributor of hosiery, who shall elucidate matters to a greater

extent and infuse greater
verisimilitude into the
narrative.

Spending

It is of utmost importance for children to acquire the ability to effectively manage their expenditures and savings in a harmonious manner. Every child derives pleasure from the expenditure of funds. And that too lavishly. There would not be a child in attendance who does not enjoy expending money. You exhaust your allowance promptly upon receiving it from your parents until it is depleted. Finances swiftly transition from abundance to scarcity, reflecting a fleeting nature akin to streaming water. In addition, you exhibit a propensity for expending finances on endeavors that will not yield advantageous outcomes in the future. Providing an allowance for your children can impose a substantial financial responsibility on your parents, particularly in the event that you do not exercise prudent spending habits. In order to circumvent the squandering of one's finances, it is necessary to acquire the skill of allocating expenditure in a particular manner. If you exercise proper fiscal management, you are more apt to develop financial responsibility during your formative years and eventually attain the bicycle that you have long considered unattainable.

When you engage in expenditures, it is unnecessary for you to engage in them solitary. Contemplate the option of dividing expenses with your acquaintances or siblings, whenever feasible, such as in the context of magazines, excursions, literature, and related items. Maximize the utilization of shared interests by effectively allocating mutually desired resources.

Additionally, endeavor to amass a substantial number of coupons and gift cards. In the event that the gift cards you have received are intended for items that you have no desire to acquire, you have the option to engage in the resale of said cards. Raise and other gift marketplaces will willingly receive them in exchange for a fee.

Arbitrage whenever possible

At its most basic level, Buffett's investment strategy can be classified into three distinct categories:

General investments. Underpriced, high-quality investments that provide a satisfactory level of security.

Controlling investment. Enterprises over which Berkshire maintains a controlling stake or complete ownership. Under certain circumstances, Buffett transitioned gradually from a broad investment approach to complete acquisition of ownership. Instances can be found in the form of the esteemed Berkshire Hathaway and the notable GEICO.

Arbitrages or special situations. Opportunities that may arise during instances of mergers, acquisitions, restructurings, liquidations, fluctuations in currency or commodity markets, among others.

"In the absence of my mother this evening, I would like to reveal to you all that I have engaged in the practice of arbitrage," stated Buffett during a professional seminar. Buffett acquired knowledge in the art of arbitrage during his formative years at Graham-Newman. Arbitrage, in its unadulterated manifestation, entails the act of acquiring goods or assets at a comparatively reduced cost in one market, subsequently offloading them at a more elevated valuation in an alternate market. Buffett utilizes arbitrage when a company discloses their intention to acquire another company at a price exceeding the prevailing market value: "We assess the arbitrage transaction upon its announcement." We evaluate their announcements, estimate its value, calculate the cost we will incur, and determine the duration of our commitment. We endeavor to ascertain the likelihood of its successful passage. The aforementioned is the computation: the specific names of the companies involved hold little significance. In the early months of 1998, Buffett disclosed that Berkshire had acquired a total of 129.7 million ounces of silver, amounting to approximately 30% of the global stockpile found above the Earth's surface.

Buffett initiated his purchasing activity on July 25th, 1997, coinciding with a day when the price of silver futures contracts plummeted to $4.32 per ounce, marking the lowest observed price in a span of 650 years. The expenditure incurred by Berkshire for the acquisition of silver amounted to $650 million. In February 1998, upon announcing the acquisition of silver, his investment had experienced an appreciation of $850 million. This represents the most substantial individual silver position witnessed since the attempted manipulation of the silver market by the Hunt brothers in the year 1980. Notwithstanding the remarkable magnitude of Buffett's accumulation, it merely constitutes approximately 2% of Berkshire's capital. Buffett initially developed an inclination towards silver during the 1960s, a pivotal period when the U.S. Government was preparing to declassify the metal as a legal tender. Despite not being the rightful owner, he diligently monitored the underlying principles of silver. Buffett and Munger concluded that a state of equilibrium would eventually reoccur and lead to a higher price, when bullion inventories significantly declined as a result of an excess in user demand compared to mine production and reclamation. Although the process of establishing equilibrium was time-consuming, it eventually reached fruition.

During the 2000 annual meeting, Munger articulated, "The journey has been lackluster." Nonetheless, silver prices gradually recovered, attaining a value of $8.83 per ounce in 2005 and $13.73 per ounce by February 2007. Over the course of a span of nine years, the value of Buffett's silver experienced a threefold increase, reaching an impressive sum of nearly $1.3 billion.

The Historical Development Of The Stock Market

It is challenging to fathom a point in history when the concept of the stock market was nonexistent. The stock market is a prevalent topic of conversation among a wide range of individuals. Even those individuals who do not partake in investment activities possess knowledge of its existence. It is widely acknowledged that the New York Stock Exchange holds the distinction of being the largest market, accommodating companies seeking global recognition. However, by what means did the stock market come into existence? Is there an alternative exchange besides the NYSE (New York Stock Exchange)? There exists a greater number of exchanges, originating from the Real Merchants of Venice and British Coffeehouses.

Europe was replete with financiers who served to bridge the gaps existing among the major banking institutions. Moneylenders would engage in exchanges among each other. A single lender may transfer a high-risk, high-interest loan to another lender as a means of disposing of it. Moneylenders, too, acquired government bonds. Through an organic process of progression, financial institutions began offering debts for purchase to individuals seeking investment opportunities.

In the 14th century, the Venetians emerged as prominent financiers, expanding their portfolio to include the acquisition and trading of government securities from diverse nations. The slates would contain detailed records regarding the debts held by the lender and the available investment opportunities.

Approximately two centuries later, the occurrence of the inaugural stock exchange took place. In Antwerp, Belgium, there existed a consortium of brokers and moneylenders who convened for the purpose of conducting negotiations with businesses, governments, and individuals. During that period, the only assets that were eligible for trading were bonds and promissory notes. The notion of paper stocks being exchanged for monetary value was non-existent. Nevertheless, there existed a reciprocal association between the business and finance sectors.

Within a span of fewer than 100 years, the emergence of the East India Companies became apparent. The Dutch,

French, and British authorities issued charters to East India companies and maintained a vested interest in the aforementioned companies. The authorities will appropriate the gains accrued from commerce with the East Indies and Asia.

Investors also allocate their capital towards the acquisition and staffing of maritime vessels. Typically, limited liability companies would embark on solitary expeditions with the aim of procuring merchandise from Asia and the East Indies, thus endeavoring to generate financial returns for the investor. Typically, fresh enterprises were established in anticipation of forthcoming voyages as a means to mitigate the perils inherent in investing in ships that could potentially encounter calamitous outcomes. The East India companies collaborated with investors through the provision of dividends derived from the merchandise they acquired. Stocks had been duly established, marking the inception of the pioneering joint stock company. During that period, the existence of royal charters rendered competition unfeasible, thereby enabling investors to accrue substantial profits.

England developed their own concept in association with the East India companies. They issued physical share certificates that could be traded among investors. It would be characterized as a transaction involving shares of stocks, albeit outside the realm of a regulated exchange. The majority of investors and brokers solely engaged in the coffee industry. Announcements regarding debt problems or the offering of shares will be displayed on the shop entrances.

Inevitably, monopolies ultimately collapse. The British East India Company possessed a governmental monopoly, thereby maintaining a competitive edge. Investors reaped substantial dividends, liquidated their shares to amass newfound wealth, and were met with a surge of interest from a multitude of other investors eager to partake in the opportunity.

It was an imperative era that necessitated the implementation of regulations to govern the issuance of shares, as a lack thereof had resulted in rampant activities devoid of any framework or oversight. The South Seas Company was established with an official charter, endorsed by the King, which mandated the compulsory sale of shares and subsequent re-issues upon their listing. New investor offices were established in London, prompting individuals to enthusiastically acquire accessible shares in various companies. Regrettably, the notion did not endure due to the SSC's inability to generate satisfactory returns on the dwindling profits it generated. The issuance of shares was prohibited by the government in response to the crashing of the SSC.

The NYSE

The London Stock Exchange was inaugurated in the year 1773 in the city of London. It implemented regulations to limit share ownership, however, it initially adhered to the SSC doctrine. After a span of nineteen years, the establishment of the New York Stock Exchange took place. It was established with the purpose of engaging in the trading of stocks. Philadelphia already possessed a stock exchange; however, the positioning of said exchange did not confer the same level of advantage as that enjoyed by the NYSE. Situated in close proximity to the harbor, amidst the influx of commercial activities directing towards North America, the New York Stock Exchange swiftly asserted its supremacy over the domain of North American stock trading.

The New York Stock Exchange retained its regulatory framework, encompassing rules, regulations, and legal provisions, although comparatively less stringent when compared to the regulations applied by the London Stock Exchange. By granting companies the ability to participate in the exchange and trade their shares, the NYSE was able to considerably enhance its position as a formidable marketplace for the sale of corporate shares.

It was not devoid of challenges. The stock market operates as a reflection of the underlying economic stability. During a period of instability, the stock market may experience a crash due to a lack of liquidity, as was the case during the Great Depression. The observation was made by all that the banks underwent a state of failure primarily attributable to mounting debt burdens and inadequate liquidity. This, consequently, inflicted hardships upon various sectors, leading to the closure of businesses and a significant decline in stock market values.

Final Thoughts

The establishment of the stock market arose due to the necessity of providing a designated platform for the exchange of shares, which was already being carried out. It is imperative for governments to exercise regulatory oversight over the sale of stocks in order to mitigate potential risks and avert incidents such as the market crash of the SSC. However, the aforementioned affluent individuals also displayed avarice. The establishment of stock exchanges arose as a result of the recognition of a distinct means to generate wealth through the utilization of another individual's work.

Does Investing In Penny Stocks Offer A Worthwhile Opportunity?

If an investment exhibits a high level of risk and necessitates additional effort to make sound investment decisions, it would be prudent to assess the viability of penny stocks as a suitable investment option. The inclusion of additional risk can render situations considerably intimidating, particularly for individuals who are inexperienced.

Undoubtedly, the most effective approach to evaluating would be to examine the benefits. Gain a comprehensive understanding of both the potential risks and benefits involved, subsequently allowing for an informed evaluation of whether the potential benefits outweigh the associated risks.

Examining both the advantages and disadvantages can foster impartiality in your decision-making process regarding trades, enabling you to navigate setbacks or losses with enhanced foresight and preparedness in the event that the risks materialize unfavorably. The potential hazards cannot be viewed as an unequivocal certainty, yet it is widely acknowledged by traders that they have experienced a considerable number of setbacks within the realm of trading. This is an integral facet of the actuality one must encounter when engaging in trading. It is highly unlikely that we will encounter smooth sailing. The volatility of the markets renders such an eventuality highly improbable.

Advantages of Penny Stocks

Initially, it is not necessary to possess a substantial account in order to commence. Given the relatively modest share prices, initiating an investment in this context may prove advantageous, especially if financial resources are currently limited. This implies that you have the opportunity to challenge societal preconceptions and initiate your investment endeavors at an early stage. Commencing your investment journey promptly is undoubtedly one of the most prudent decisions you can make. The passage of time serves as a valuable asset in the realm of investments.

Hard work and extensive research will be duly recognized and rewarded. If one acquires proficiency in the art of researching and uncovering information pertaining to penny stocks, the subsequent stages of their investment expedition shall be remarkably alleviated. Conducting thorough research and exercising prudence is a fundamental strategy in the field of investing, cultivating the distinction between an uninformed investor and a knowledgeable one. Across all literary publications, online resources, and even auditory digital media platforms dedicated to the subject of investments, it is highly improbable that one would encounter any instance where individuals advocate refraining from conducting thorough personal research. Relying on the information or assertions of others, particularly on social media platforms, is an ill-advised decision. However, it is worth noting that witnessing the fruits of your labor being duly acknowledged can indeed be regarded as a benefit.

One can observe an imminent potential for profit, whether it be ascending or descending, at a significantly accelerated pace compared to conventional stocks. With regard to penny stocks, one can realize gains or losses from fluctuations in their value. By implementing a short selling strategy, it is feasible to generate a financial gain even in the event that the value of a penny stock experiences a decline. Short selling represents the polar opposite of a conventional and customary stock investment.

Additionally, there is the favorable aspect of potential profit, as penny stocks constitute smaller enterprises with the capability of expanding. A notable benefit for individuals commencing their investment journey is the opportunity to witness modest investments flourish and yield substantial returns over time. Ultimately, the pursuit of financial gains stands as a significant incentive in investment endeavors. Given the existence of increased risks, the potential for greater rewards can serve as a incentive to contemplate engaging in investments. Assuming you have a higher propensity for risk, given the persistent possibility of adverse outcomes. This benefit is linked to an essential piece of guidance: Refrain from investing in assets that you cannot afford to lose. This piece of advice will serve as a protective measure in the event of a significant setback.

While it may pose a challenge to monitor the progress of the research, it is certainly within the realm of feasibility to track the velocity of price fluctuations. Indeed, one shall observe the fluctuations in price within a short span of days. This option is particularly suited for individuals who prefer a proactive approach when it comes to managing investments. Day trading is a widely employed approach in penny stock investments, thereby rendering this aspect significantly conducive and pragmatic to execute day trading activities. The sole determinant lies in acquiring the ability to discern and monitor the recurrent patterns associated with the fluctuations in price.

Due to the comparatively lower prices, purchasing a diverse range of stocks becomes more feasible. By introducing diversity into your portfolio, you mitigate risks and substantially enhance your likelihood of achieving success. This objective can also be achieved, particularly with regards to investments of shorter durations. Frequently, when dealing with sizable traders that undergo swift alterations, the chances of affording a diverse range of options are minimal. This can be effortlessly achieved in the context of low-value stocks. It can also yield a predominantly favorable impact on your investment portfolio. Typically, financial professionals prioritize an individual's long-term investments; nonetheless, they recognize the significance of maintaining a well-diversified portfolio.

Including penny stocks in your portfolio can also enhance your liquidity and diversify the range of stocks within your holdings. This undoubtedly enhances the overall value of your portfolio. Various factors that have the potential to enhance your investment portfolio can confer significant benefits, and it is entirely feasible to derive substantial profits solely from engaging in penny stock investment. While it is advisable to diversify one's investment portfolio, there exists significant potential to achieve diversity within a penny stock and subsequently derive financial gains from such diversification. Granted, if you effectively employ optimal strategies, promptly address any setbacks, and gradually accumulate significant victories,

Additionally, a notable advantage exists in terms of exposure, particularly in terms of establishing connections with other firms, given that numerous large enterprises frequently invest in low-priced stocks. This is an auspicious indication, since not only does it facilitate networking, but the act of companies investing in penny stocks serves as an epitome of the latent prospects they hold. Individuals with experience in the professional realm are well aware that increased visibility consistently yields favorable outcomes. Being cognizant of other enterprises and cultivating professional relationships, particularly if you are professionally engaged in the corporate realm, can enable you to develop a comprehensive understanding of the financial markets. This confers a significant advantage, considering that with sufficient practice and effort, one can consistently stay ahead of the norm. The knowledge obtained from investing in penny stocks can also be advantageous in conventional investment endeavors. Despite the disparity, engaging in penny stock trading imparts essential qualities such as resilience and the aptitude to conduct comprehensive research under limited means. After gaining experience with penny stocks, you may discover that investing in regular stocks becomes even more effortless. That also confers a significant benefit.

The Integration Of Facebook Into The Metaverse And Nfts

Mark Zuckerberg made a recent declaration of Facebook's rebranding as Meta. The purpose of this rebranding initiative is to strategically realign the company's image with its newfound aspiration of becoming the foremost metaverse company.

NFTs refer to digital assets whose ownership is authenticated and recorded on the blockchain, typically the Ethereum network.

It is evident from the statements made by Zuckerberg and the members of the Facebook team that their purpose is to establish themselves as the metaverse platform. Such a development carries significant consequences for the trajectory of non-fungible tokens, particularly if Facebook achieves its objective. Michelle Shaw, the appointed executive overseeing metaverse products at Facebook, conveyed their intentions to streamline the process of selling non-fungible tokens (NFTs) and facilitate the establishment of entrepreneurial ventures within the metaverse.

Taking into account the key points discussed in the Facebook Connect keynote, we would like to draw attention to the specific markets within Facebook's envisioned metaverse where Non-Fungible Tokens (NFTs) are poised to hold a substantial influence.

Virtual representations and accessories for virtual representations

Zuckerberg emphasized that the metaverse serves as a mechanism to facilitate human connectivity. In contrast to our existing web 2.0 configuration, establishing digital connections entails presenting oneself through digital avatars. In order to portray your visual identity in three-dimensional form, it is necessary to utilize avatars.

Avatars possess the capacity to represent your facial and bodily features through real-time volumetric scanning. They have the capacity to be animated or possessing a cartoon-like appearance, hyper-realistic, or entirely fantastical in nature.

Although it may appear inconceivable that an avatar can be perceived as a digital possession subject to purchase and trade, there exists a significant potential for enterprises capable of devising methods to create highly lifelike non-fungible token avatars capturing individuals at specific instances.

Digital clothing

The potential scale of the NFT market pertaining to appearance-related NFTs will be substantial. It is apparent that companies such as Dress X and reputable designer brands have already entered this domain.

Virtual environments represented as non-fungible tokens (NFTs)

Zuckerberg also insinuated in his keynote address that the architecture of the virtual realms themselves could potentially be commodified, collected, and exchanged by individuals. During the main address, they assemble within a suspended spatial cuboid. This particular category of non-fungible tokens holds significant allure due to its capability of facilitating collective experiences. It does not embody the characteristics of a mere work of art or a digital card to be idly displayed; rather, it serves as a platform for social interaction and fostering connections with fellow individuals.

Events

Artists possess the opportunity to market NFT tokens which enable supporters to gain entry to either a physical concert, a virtual concert, or an augmented reality rendition of the event. Additional options could include a gathering, an online celebration, and so forth. This arrangement could also be suitable for sporting occasions such as the Super Bowl.

The creator economy

Content creators have the ability to utilize Non-Fungible Tokens (NFTs) as a means of establishing a connection with their respective audiences and fostering the expansion of their entrepreneurial endeavors. Tokens can serve as a means to patronize the creator and grant aficionados exclusive opportunities to partake in limited events and gain early access to content such as music or videos.

Gaming

NFTs and their association with gaming are inseparable topics of discussion. During the keynote address, Zuckerberg made the announcement that The Quest 2 will offer a rendition of GTA. He refrained from disclosing the availability of NFT items within the game, however, the potential tokenization of in-game items in GTA showcases the possibility of immense growth for this conventional gaming platform.

We are pioneers in the nascent realm of NFTs and the metaverse. It will take approximately a time span of five to ten years before widespread adoption is achieved. Several prerequisites must be met before we reach our desired destination, including:

Metaverse hardware: A headset is imperative. Currently, our inventory includes the oculus headset; however, there is a requirement for a headset that ensures optimal wearer comfort during extended periods.

Metaverse software framework: It is imperative to establish a robust infrastructure and establish interconnections among metaverse applications. Currently, we have discerned distinct metaverses such as Decentraland, Roblox, and the Sandbox. One has the option to individually visit each location, although it is not feasible to travel on foot between them. However, it is imperative to establish this level of connectivity on a larger, more comprehensive scale. These various individual applications are facilitating the adoption process and acquainting individuals with the intricacies and ethos of the metaverse, encompassing the utilization of NFTs.

Establishing A Novel Persona In The Metaverse

As previously established, the metaverse permeates our surroundings and shall persist indefinitely so long as there are virtual developers dedicated to the ongoing creation of virtual realms akin to second life. Whenever you access the internet to monitor the interactions occurring within your various social media platforms, you are effectively immersing yourself in the digital manifestation of your personal sphere. Facebook and analogous social media platforms serve as manifestations of a virtual reality environment that mirrors our own reality. The concept of the Metaverse centers around the formation of a novel persona, and it can be observed that numerous individuals maintain distinct representations of themselves across the various social media platforms they engage with regularly. In formal tone, you could rephrase the sentence as follows: "There exists a persona of oneself that is recognized within the confines of the workplace, and conceivably, another persona emerges when engaging in activities such as waiting in line at the bank to access internet banking or procuring a visa through the use of one's passport."

You partake in the use of Instagram, a platform through which you selectively curate information to conceal aspects of yourself that you find undesirable for public consumption. On certain occasions, it is desirable for individuals to openly share their enjoyment of life. They may choose to showcase their culinary prowess by uploading images of recently baked cookies, or commemorate special moments such as their children's birthdays by capturing shared photographs and extending heartfelt birthday wishes.

The demeanor you exhibit within a professional setting embodies a polished and refined image while incorporating industry-specific jargon and expressions in the English language. You make use of various communication tools such as email, Zoom, Slack, Google Meets, Asana, and similar platforms. There exists a representation of yourself on Facebook where you present yourself by posing and smiling with a cake or beverage, regularly share quotes, and even post a photograph of yourself, most likely accompanied by your canine companion, during a recreational stroll. You also exchange various humorous memes with your acquaintances.

In the realm of the metaverse, our identities assume disparate forms. It is uncommon for individuals to exhibit identical behavior in both their online and offline personas. Frequently, the representation of your authentic self in online spaces diverges from your offline persona. These distinct iterations are typically associated with differing variants of your name, and the manner of communication often differs from the formal discourse observed in professional settings. Various personas can serve as your representation in the digital realm.

Avatars serve as the contemporary manifestations of our online personas within the metaverse.

Could you kindly explain the meaning of the term 'Avatar'?

Upon encountering the term "Avatar," one may often visualize an image resembling that of a Sims character or a cartoon-like representation. Additionally, there exist more profound and emblematic depictions of Avatar.

NFTs will serve the purpose of generating digital profile images comprising of characters and their randomly assigned attributes, facilitated by the algorithm. Each NFT is distinctive, serving as our virtual counterparts within the metaverse. The NTFS showcases authentic digital artwork. You have the opportunity to possess your own Avatar, allowing for easy identification and fostering a sense of individuality within the metaverse. You have the opportunity to obtain exclusive commercial rights for the Avatar. One can also accrue digital currency such as cryptocurrency. One can demonstrate their elevated standing in the metaverse by exhibiting expertise and deep knowledge in the field of cryptocurrencies. One can authentically express themselves. One may choose to portray oneself as an idealized or aspirational embodiment when offering oneself for a specific undertaking.

The concept of Digital Identity, emerging as the new representation of individuals within the metaverse, will continue to be a prominent subject of discussion for an extended period. We have been cultivating our online personas for several years. With each new application, game development, or virtual world creation, we undertake the process of establishing a fresh persona from scratch. Over the course of the last two decades, individuals have established virtual personas. Numerous individuals have garnered significant attention and gained popularity on platforms like Instagram, TikTok, as well as through the circulation and dissemination of humorous memes, among other avenues. However, in the event that one encounters these renowned individuals in person, it is highly probable that they may go unrecognized. They largely deviate from the image they project of themselves.

The metaverse enables us to establish a consistent and unalterable identity which can be employed universally. The metaverse affords us an unparalleled opportunity for self-expression and emancipates us from the mundanities of daily existence. One can attain accomplishments that are beyond reach in reality. In actuality, the process of constructing your professional trajectory, enterprise, or brand can span a considerable number of years. However, within the realm of the metaverse, such objectives can be achieved with remarkable ease. In the event that the reputation of a brand is irreparably tarnished in the physical world, it has the potential to permanently harm your image, whereas the metaverse offers the opportunity to redeem and reconstruct oneself.

Virtual Reality

Virtual reality is predominantly employed to denote various immersive engagements, encompassing augmented reality, extended reality, and mixed reality. Virtual reality is a fabricated, all-encompassing digital reality that generates an environment wherein users can engage, albeit without tangible existence. The virtual reality environments are primarily novel in nature; nonetheless, they are designed to bear resemblance to their counterparts in the tangible world. They invariably possess unique attributes.

Virtual reality utilizes computer technology to construct a simulated environment. In the realm of virtual reality, the individual actively engages with the game world instead of passively observing it on a screen. The users will experience a high level of immersion within the virtual environment, enabling them to engage and interact with the various elements and individuals present, thus providing a tangible sensory experience.

Fundamental language and principles

Head-mounted optical device or HMOD

This term is widely recognized and frequently encountered when one engages in literature regarding virtual reality. The Head-Mounted Displays (HMDs) represent the latest iteration of hardware designed to provide users with immersive Virtual Reality (VR) experiences. It bears resemblance to a helmet or goggles, and can be secured around your face or seated atop your head. Certain devices are equipped with sensors designed to monitor the movement of the user's head.

Head tracking

Head tracking refers to the utilization of sensors that monitor and sustain the movement of an individual's head. This mechanism concurrently adjusts the displayed images to correspondingly align with the direction in which the head is turned. In any location you orient your head, a visual interface will be visible. An exemplary illustration of head tracking can be found in the Oculus Rift. When the Oculus Rift is being worn, it facilitates the head tracking functionality which enables the user to orient their gaze in any direction - right, left, down, or up - while maintaining the ability to view the buildings in whichever direction they are facing.

Eye-tracking

Eye-tracking is akin to head tracking in nature; however, it diverges by detecting the precise position of the user's eyes instead of detecting the position of their head. To provide an example, let us consider a scenario where the integration of a FOVE (Foveated Rendering) technology in your head tracking detector enables the incorporation of your eyes into the headset. As a result, you would be able to effortlessly aim your weapon at a desired target simply by redirecting your gaze in the intended direction.

Visual perspective" or "scope of vision.

The field of view pertains to the angular extent within the visual field. Having a wide field of view is of paramount importance, as it greatly enhances the user's sense of immersion and presence in the virtual reality experience. In order to mitigate ocular fatigue, it is advisable to maintain the viewing angle at approximately 200 degrees. The greater the magnitude of the angle, the more enriched and captivating the experience becomes.

Latency

Latency refers to a phenomenon whereby there is a noticeable delay in the occurrence or response of a particular event or process. During the course of virtual reality exploration, one may observe a delay in the synchronization of visual elements as they turn their head towards a specific direction. (Therefore, a delay has been experienced.) It generally constitutes an unfavorable encounter, and such occurrences are not commonly observed in reality. Given that the virtual realm serves as a representation of the real world, the concept of latency is not intended to be encountered.

Simulator sickness

Simulator sickness manifests as a discrepancy between the physiological response of the body and the cognitive processing of the brain. The sensation of nausea manifests specifically during gameplay. The human mind exhibits an awareness of toxic substances, compelling the body to expel them via the process of vomiting. In order to mitigate the occurrence of simulator sickness, it is advisable to ascertain the most effective strategies for personal adaptation. If you are prone to experiencing adverse sensations when engaging in activities involving flight or leaping, it would be advisable to abstain from attempting such endeavors.

Refresh rate

The refresh rate denotes the speed at which the images undergo updates over time. As the refresh rate increases, the lag decreases in direct proportion. When uninterrupted fluidity is achieved, your immersion in the Virtual World will be enhanced, thereby minimizing the likelihood of experiencing feelings of nausea.

Haptics

Haptics refers to the somatosensory perception of touch and the resulting tactile feedback. It entails the sensation of tactile interaction within the virtual realm, wherein one perceives the act of touching an object that does not exist in tangible reality.

Presence

Once a user is able to successfully log into the virtual reality platform and become fully engrossed in the stunning digital environments, the phenomenon of presence becomes evident and influential. Achieving presence is attained at that juncture. It signifies your presence within the realm of virtual reality.

Method Eleven: Selling Cupcakes

Who among us does not derive pleasure from indulging in a delectable cupcake? If you possess a natural talent for baking, you have the opportunity to leverage your skills to generate income.

• It is imperative to ascertain whether your jurisdiction grants you the authorization to publicly sell your baked goods. Acquire the requisite licenses or permits, as they frequently become necessary in instances where you are subject to imposed limitations.

According to our bakers, custom cake orders have seen a noticeable surge during the holiday season, a time when individuals are preoccupied with various events and lack sufficient time to bake on their own.

• Undertake a comprehensive examination of your immediate competitors. When selecting a site for your bakery, particularly if your focus is on cupcake sales, it is crucial to assess areas with a limited presence of established cupcake shops. Prior to making a costly commitment, it is advised to conduct a comprehensive investigation of the pricing strategies employed by competitors in your locale, in addition to their existing assortment of cakes. Employ scholarly inquiry to ascertain the distinctiveness of your cupcake venture.

• Devote careful consideration to the recipes and enhance them further. It is imperative to possess well-refined recipes and the capacity to replicate them in order to generate revenue from the sale of cupcakes. In order to captivate a large clientele base for your ice cream, consider experimenting with a diverse range of flavors and innovative presentation styles. As an illustration, one could create cupcakes resembling the beloved characters adored by the children while incorporating flavors that resonate with their individual preferences.

• Acquire baking utensils for culinary purposes. In order to prepare the cupcakes, it will be necessary to acquire cupcake pans, pastry bags, various types of sugars, food colorings, sprinkles, mixers, refrigerated units, mixing bowls, baking ovens, cupcake liners, and so forth.

• It is advisable that you establish a blog. Conduct thorough market research and establish a blog centered around cupcakes as a strategic approach to enhance brand visibility. Request the engagement of readers in initiating a discussion on the subject of their preferred cupcake flavors. Enhance the visibility of your creations through the provision of recipes, sample portions, or exclusive promotions.

Presented below is a fail-safe recipe for delectable chocolate cupcakes that is guaranteed to captivate and delight even the most discerning palates.

Ingredients

Approximately 114 grams of sifted all-purpose flour, equal to one cup.

Please incorporate 45 grams of unsweetened natural cocoa powder, equivalent to 1/2 cup.

A quantity equivalent to three quarters of a teaspoon of baking powder.

1/2 teaspoon baking powder.

One-fourth teaspoon salt

Two eggs

Half a cup of granulated sugar

100g light brown sugar

A quantity equivalent to one third of a cup, specifically 80 milliliters, of vegetable or canola oil.

A quantity of two tablespoons of vanilla extract, which is made entirely of 100% pure vanilla.

An amount of 125 milliliters of buttermilk at room temperature.

Any type of adornment placed atop, such as Chocolate Buttercream or Vanilla Buttercream

Instructions

• Adjust the oven temperature to 350 degrees Fahrenheit (177 degrees Celsius) in order to facilitate the baking process. Prepare a muffin pan by placing liners in the cupcake compartments. Prepare an additional pan equipped with two baking sheets, as this particular recipe is expected to produce approximately 14 cupcakes.

Combine all of the dry ingredients in a large basin, ensuring thorough mixing. Combine the eggs, sugar, oil, and vanilla in a medium bowl and whisk until fully integrated.

● Divide the moist components in half and incorporate them into the mixture of dry ingredients. Proceed with adding half of the buttermilk, subsequently followed by a combination of salt and pepper. Gently stir for a brief duration.

● Utilize the remaining wet ingredients and buttermilk to complete the tasks at hand. Ensure thorough incorporation without excessive agitation or overworking. The consistency of the batter will be more viscous.

• Place the batter into the baking cups. Prevent any spills or submerging by ensuring the container is filled only to half capacity. (Do not overfill!)

• Put it in the oven and cook for a duration of 18-21 minutes, or until a toothpick can be inserted and removed without any residue remaining. Allow the product to undergo a sufficient cooling period prior to applying the frosting.

• Enhance the appearance by adorning with sprinkles, as desired. It is advisable to store leftovers in a refrigerator for a maximum duration of 5 days.

Passive Investment Funds

Given the preceding discussion on investment, there exist a multitude of paths one can pursue. Numerous investors have the capability to generate substantial financial gains effortlessly even while they are asleep. These individuals exhibit a profound understanding of their activities and possess the keen ability to exploit market conditions for their benefit. They possess extensive expertise and have garnered significant experience throughout their tenure. Certainly, there exists a considerable number of seasoned investors who continue to encounter challenges in achieving substantial financial gains. Numerous inexperienced investors typically initiate at a cautious pace and subsequently progress further. Certain individuals maintain a conservative outlook throughout their entire lifetimes. In this book, we shall operate under the premise that you possess a novice level of investment experience. Considering this factor, we shall present to you a secure methodology for entering the market in order to generate additional income via passive investment funds.

Passive investing is an investment approach employed to optimize profits through the minimization of transaction activity. In a comprehensive manner, it pertains to a purchase and retain tactic for extended timeframes. The techniques employed in this particular investment strategy are designed to circumvent the costs and constraints associated with frequent trading, which are inherent to active investment strategies. The primary premise underlying the implementation of passive investment strategies is that the market will consistently exhibit favorable returns over an extended period. They do not depend on transient variations. Passive investment funds provide a secure means of entering the realm of investing.

Active Investing

Prior to delving deeper into the intricacies of passive investment strategies, we shall proceed to elucidate the nature and characteristics of active funds. As you acquire greater ease and confidence as an investor, this approach may be one you can consider in subsequent times. Active funds necessitate a heightened level of human involvement, notably through the presence of fund managers who diligently oversee these investments and possess the ability to promptly execute decisions. Individuals and companies adhering to the active strategy maintain the belief that they possess the ability to accurately predict market movements and surpass its performance.

Active management endeavors to generate superior and expeditious returns in comparison to passive funds. The methods in question pose a considerable challenge in terms of mastery, and as previously mentioned, even the most seasoned investors encounter considerable difficulty in doing so. There are several benefits associated with active management, which include:

Benefiting from the leadership of a manager who possesses deep expertise in a specific sector, such as the automotive industry.

There exists a degree of flexibility in the investment opportunities available for acquisition, and the facility to engage in buying and selling transactions as required is readily accessible. The timing of market fluctuations plays a significant role in this.

There exists the potential for acquiring higher amounts of financial resources within a relatively brief timeframe.

These particular funds offer a multitude of benefits.

In general, active fund management encompasses a more assertive investment strategy that bears the possibility of yielding higher returns, albeit accompanied by elevated risks. The outcomes in this context are contingent upon the competencies of the individual investor or manager.

Being Aware Of The Current Developments In The Cryptocurrency Market.

A crucial aspect to ponder in relation to contemporary cryptocurrency market trends pertains to the adherence of influential cryptocurrency investors.

5.1 Precisely, what do crypto whales signify?

Crypto whales refer to both individuals and organizations that possess a substantial volume of a particular cryptocurrency's tokens or coins. While there may not exist an authoritative benchmark for designating someone as a whale, the quantity of 1,000 bitcoins is commonly referenced as the prevailing standard. Due to the considerably smaller market capitalizations of altcoins compared to that of Bitcoin, this value tends to be significantly greater.

5.2 What is the most effective method for monitoring the movements of a whale?

The subsequent factors may aid you in ascertaining the methodology for monitoring prominent individuals or entities in the cryptocurrency sphere.

Resources for monitoring cetacean species

Every node possessing a comprehensive replica of a blockchain has the capacity to scrutinize all transactions and other data elements contained within said blockchain, facilitating diverse methods of search and display.

If you have a desire to gain insights into the most prominent wallet addresses in relation to the quantity of Ethereum they possess, Etherscan can be utilized as an Ethereum-dedicated blockchain investigation tool.

Blockchain explorers

Blockchain explorers can serve as databases that enable the scrutiny of transactions, wallet identifiers, and historical data spanning from the inception of blockchains.

Etherscan, an exploratory platform for Ethereum, has the capability to display a plethora of diverse data points such as the most significant accounts based on their accumulated ETH holdings.

Nevertheless, exchanges frequently comprise the majority of the highest coin holders. This information will be unveiled in the Name Tag field.

Locations lacking proper identification and exhibiting a minimal volume of transactions are the focal points of activity. In the Ethereum mainnet, it is possible to access any wallet address and retrieve comprehensive information regarding their token holdings, including the exact quantity of tokens owned and the most recent transfer activity, among other relevant details.

You have the option of utilizing Etherscan's watchlist tool to set up alerts for monitoring transactions associated with a specific whale wallet, in case it presents a certain level of interest or curiosity, as exemplified in the following illustration.

Whale Alert

There exists a Twitter account by the name of "Whale Alert" which documents noteworthy transactions spanning different blockchains and establishes associations with widely recognized wallet addresses.

Paid platforms for conducting on-chain data analytics

In recent years, there has been a notable emergence of specialized, fee-based analytics systems that undertake all necessary tasks on behalf of their clientele, granting them access to a diverse array of advanced metrics and filtering options.

CryptoQuant and Glassnode are highly renowned sources that offer customizable metrics.

Monitor the activities of the whales while simultaneously devising individualized strategies.

Whale monitoring could aid in your understanding and contextualization of market fluctuations and patterns. Nevertheless, it is advisable to refrain from utilizing such tactics as the sole basis for all investment and trading decisions.

An Informative Handbook On The Investment Strategies Of Mutual Funds

According to renowned entrepreneur Warren Buffett, the esteemed pioneer behind the establishment of the Berkshire Hathaway Mutual Fund, as mentioned on the official website www.flickr.com.

A mutual fund consists of funds that have been contributed by individual investors, corporations, and other financial entities. A mutual fund corporation engages the services of a "portfolio manager" with the goal of augmenting the capital invested by the shareholders.

The Advantages Offered by Mutual Funds

- Dissolution – Shareholders of mutual funds possess the capacity to effectively recover their initial invested funds.

Generally, they have the ability to promptly sell off their mutual fund investments, without experiencing significant declines in their market worth. However, it is imperative that you consider the potential charges that may be imposed on your transactions.

- Skilled Oversight - By investing in mutual funds, you are benefitting from the expertise of a skilled financial manager. - Proficient Administration - Through the investment in mutual funds, you are gaining advantages from the proficiency of a knowledgeable financial administrator. - Expert Management - By investing in mutual funds, you are availing the services of a proficient financial manager. This person will meticulously distribute your funds across carefully scrutinized assets. This implies that you will be liberated from the responsibility of dedicating your time and energy to meticulously examining companies for potential investment opportunities, as a proficient manager will assume this responsibility in your stead.

- Portfolio diversification is of utmost importance for investors of all types, as explained in the preceding chapters. It possesses the capacity to mitigate your losses and maximize your potential profits. The acquisition of a mutual fund will swiftly confer diversification onto your investment portfolio. Asset managers strategically distribute the existing capital among a diverse range of companies and industries, thereby mitigating potential financial adversities for their investors.

Choosing the Ideal Mutual Fund Company:

Delineate your objectives and risk tolerance – It is crucial to determine your intended results and goals prior to acquiring shares in a mutual fund. Do you have a primary aim of attaining sustainable and enduring financial profitability? Are you satisfied with the current level of income that you are earning? Do you have any intentions to allocate your financial resources towards the expenses associated with your pursuit of higher education? Are you inclined towards ensuring the stability of your financial situation, particularly for the purpose of retirement?

Furthermore, it is of utmost importance to take into account your ability to tolerate risk. Do you possess a propensity for assuming financial risks by investing in ventures characterized by high levels of risk? What are the prescribed standards for allowable losses within your organization? Do you have a preference for the financial manager to exercise prudence in managing your funds?

Determine the suitable investment strategy and mutual fund classification that corresponds with your financial goals - If your aim is to distribute your assets over a prolonged duration and you are open to assuming significant risks, it is recommended to search for a mutual fund that prioritizes long-term capital appreciation. Companies falling within this particular category often allocate their funds in the stock market. Therefore, these entities are considered to be extremely precarious investment instruments.

In the event that you seek prompt returns, it is recommended to consider obtaining shares from a fund classified as an "income" fund. These mutual fund firms often prioritize their focus on corporate liabilities and government bonds.

Kindly examine the relevant fees and charges - Mutual fund companies generate proceeds through the imposition of fees on their investors. Hence, it is crucial that you possess an extensive comprehension of the diverse fees that you may potentially come across.

Certain companies enforce a "load fee," which includes a transaction fee that is imposed when buying or selling an investment. The charges associated with the purchase of an investment are commonly known as "front-end load fees," while the charges levied upon the sale are referred to as "back-end load fees." It is customary for these fees to comprise approximately 4% to 6% of the investment's overall value. Mutual fund firms implement these fees to address the expenses linked with investment management and to discourage excessive client transactions.

It is generally recommended to actively seek mutual fund companies that provide investment options without any accompanying load fees. These companies refrain from placing any front-end or back-end charges on their investors. On the contrary, they may levy supplementary charges such as administrative fees, management expense ratios, and analogous expenses.

Assess the extent of the company's influence - By and large, the financial success of the mutual fund company is not hindered by its size. However, certain circumstances arise in which the organization becomes excessively expansive. The Magellan Fund offered by Fidelity is a prime illustration of this concept. At the commencement of the 21st century, the monetary assets of this corporation eventually reached a total of $100 billion. The organization was compelled to modify its investment strategies and protocols due to a significant inflow of funds. As a result, it experienced a significant decline in both its operational effectiveness and financial viability.

Evaluate the Manager's capability and past performance – Since the fund manager will be responsible for managing your hard-earned capital, it is crucial to determine their proficiency. You are welcome to authenticate his qualifications and delve into his professional background at different organizations. Moreover, it is crucial that you engage in extensive individual investigation concerning the manager's historical performance. Provided herewith is a curated collection of questions that can potentially aid you in facilitating this endeavor:

Has the manager achieved results that correspond with the overall performance of the market?

- Did the assets display higher levels of volatility relative to the market indices? - Were the assets more prone to volatility in comparison to the market indices? - Did the assets demonstrate increased volatility when compared to the market indices? - Did the assets manifest greater volatility in contrast to the market indices? - Were the assets subject to heightened levels of volatility as opposed to the market indices?

Has the manager attained diverse levels of investment returns?

Has the mutual fund company experienced a significant level of turnover that is considered unfavorable?

These pieces of information are of substantial significance. However, it is imperative to acknowledge that previous results do not assure future consequences.

Easy Investing Math

Before we commence, kindly refrain from being intimidated by the term "mathematics." It is indeed quite straightforward, contrary to the misrepresentation of your high school teacher. We will solely focus on the essential principles of value investing, without delving into any other aspects. You will not be required to handle formulas containing non-English alphabets. That's a guarantee.

The Concept of Temporal Monetary Worth

In the context of commerce, the principle enunciated by the King can be understood as the concept of the time value of money. In order to elucidate this concept further, it is essential to note that the value of a dollar in your grandfather's era is markedly distinct from its present worth, and it is certain that its value will continue to differ in the future as well. Firstly, the issue of depreciation must be considered. Conversely, through the process of investing funds, it will progressively appreciate in value. It pertains to understanding its capacity for appreciation, and the extent to which it manifests.

Present Value vs. Future Value

Suppose you were to allocate a sum of $100 towards investment. The current value amounts to $100. As time progresses, suppose that your investment experiences growth. The anticipated amount in the future would be $100, inclusive of the accumulated returns over a period of time. When funds are invested, they experience compounding, resulting in the growth of the initial principal amount of $100, along with the cumulative returns obtained on that initial amount. One can ascertain the potential growth of this by calculating the rate of return within a specific time frame. This is where compounding formulas offer a solution.

Suppose an individual informs you that they intend to provide you with a sum of $100 within the span of the upcoming five years. This does not imply that you have gained an additional $100 in wealth, as the funds have not been physically received by you at present. Suppose your objective is to accumulate a sum of $100 within a span of five years. In such a scenario, the sole means of achieving this would involve allocating a portion of the present amount towards investment, and subsequently exercising patience to receive the anticipated returns. The future valuation of that segment will be contingent upon the passage of time and the rate of return. State the percentage of return as being 10 percent. This implies that you would need to contribute approximately $62.10 in order to accumulate a sum of $100 upon the termination of the five-year timeframe. So, how can you effectively utilize these strategies in your favor? Instead of passively holding onto your funds and speculating on their future value, it is advisable to contemplate the steps necessary to cultivate and expand your wealth with the objective of reaching the desired sum of $100 within a five-year timeframe.

The Compounding Formula

Referred to as the time value of money equation, the compounding formula bestows a substantial amount of information to individuals engaged in value investing. It is imperative to possess not only a thorough knowledge of the formula, but also a deep comprehension of its underlying mechanisms, functionality, and the predominant factors that influence it. The compounding equation alone is insufficient for achieving success as a value investor, however, it is undeniably paramount. Similar to the essential addition of salt to enhance the flavor of a dish. Here is the prescribed equation:

The future value (FV) can be calculated by multiplying the present value (PV) by the product of one plus the interest rate (i) raised to the power of n, the number of periods.

Where...

FV represents the anticipated monetary worth at a later point in time.

The present value can be defined as PV.

I represents the rate of interest or return.

N represents the duration of the investment in years.

Analyzing the equation: The forthcoming worth, referred to as FV, essentially relies on the present worth, known as PV, which is magnified or extended by the interest rate throughout the passage of time. The interest for a one-year period can be determined by multiplying the present value by one, representing the actual value, and subsequently adding the interest rate i. This calculation yields the anticipated value at a future point.

If an interest calculation is required for a duration exceeding one year, it is necessary to multiply the present value by (1 i), taking into account the specific time period. Therefore, when determining the interest over a span of five years, it is necessary to iterate the present value by continuously multiplying it with the interest rate plus 1. Given an initial investment of $100, compounded at an annual interest rate of 10 percent over a period of five years, the resulting calculations would be as follows:

The future value (FV) can be determined by multiplying $100 by the factor of 1 plus 0.1, raised to the power of 5.

Or

$100 x (1.61)

Or

$161.0

When determining the present value, the equation would appear as follows:

The equation "PV = FV ÷ (1 + i)^n"

In order to ascertain the interest rate, the following calculation can be used:

The equation can be expressed in a more formal tone as follows: "I can be determined by subtracting 1 from the multiplication of (the quotient obtained by dividing the future value by the present value) and (1 divided by the number of periods)."

In order to determine the value of n, logarithmic calculations would be necessary.

The significance of the time value of money lies in its capacity to enable the determination of the potential worth of an investment over time in the foreseeable future. There exist specific value investing techniques that necessitate the process of discounting, which involves ascertaining the present value of future income streams. The consideration of the time value holds significance while evaluating your investment's worth and conducting comparisons with alternative options.

Your Fulfillment Of The Agreement

In the realm of existence, the sole indisputable realities encompass the inevitability of mortality and the obligation of taxation. You are indeed required to fulfill your tax obligations on your investments; however, the taxation mechanisms for investments diverge considerably from those applicable to your regular income. The amount of your current tax liability will fluctuate considerably based on several factors, including your income, the state in which you reside, and your employment status as an independent contractor. If you qualify, it is possible to avail the earned income tax credit, whereas, as a contractor, you might be required to fulfill your own tax obligations. Given your investments, it would be prudent for you to redirect a greater degree of focus towards your taxes, as forthcoming alterations are imminent.

To begin with, there exists a fundamental regulation governing the taxation principles associated with investments within the United States. If an investment is retained for a period of one year or more, the tax liability experiences a marked decrease. This operates via a mechanism known as the capital gains tax, which encompasses two variations, namely short-term and long-term capital gains. The system has undergone notable transformations over the years, and at present, discussions are underway in the capital regarding further modifications to the tax rate, even as you peruse this literature. Presently, the prevailing mechanism dictates that any investment yielding profits within a span of less than one year is deemed a part of your taxable income. For instance, in the event that an individual's annual income is $40,000 and they generate a profit of $5,000 from the stock market within a year, this would result in a combined taxable income amounting to $45,000. The impact of this will be particularly pronounced among individuals with higher incomes compared to those with lower incomes. Nevertheless, individuals earning $25,000 annually who receive an additional $5,000 from stock market investments should anticipate becoming ineligible for certain government assistance programs. Please bear in mind this point when you liquidate your investments.

Fortunately, there exists the provision of the long-term capital gains tax, whereby returns on investments are subject to a maximum tax rate of 20%, exclusively applicable to individuals in the uppermost echelons of the tax bracket. For the majority of readers of this literature, it is probable that the range lies within 0% and 15%. If your tax bracket falls within the range of 0% to 15%, long-term capital gains are subject to a taxation rate of zero dollars. For instance, in the event that an individual's annual income is $25,000, it can be anticipated that there will be no tax imposition on a $5,000 profit generated from the sale of stocks. This aspect serves as a significant distinguishing factor when it comes to your taxation obligations, and it is advisable to retain your investments for a full year in order to mitigate the tax implications associated with immediate capital gains. In addition to the fact that many Americans are not liable for any taxes on this income, it also has the effect of lowering their income bracket compared to if they had earned profits in the initial year. The significant implications of potential increases in your overall tax burden and the potential loss of certain government benefits provide considerable weight to the attractiveness of the long-term capital gains tax.

Furthermore, apart from aspiring to retain your investments for a duration of one year or more, it is imperative to take into account the potential deductions applicable to your investments. To illustrate, in the event that any of your investments fail to yield profit, you have the potential to carry forward that tax amount in order to augment your maximum deduction. It is advisable to consult an accountant for optimal implementation, however, the underlying concept is that, until your investments generate profits, any losses incurred, whether recognized or not, can be utilized as deductions on your tax returns. These deductions can be carried forward for several years as well, meaning that if some of your investments generate income while others do not, the losses incurred by the non-profitable investment will be applied as deductions on your tax forms, provided that it does not eventually result in a profit.

In the preceding chapter, you acquired knowledge regarding non-traditional investment strategies. These investments were significantly more personalized and did not involve major institutional players. Please be advised that it is imperative to bear in mind that these investments must be disclosed on your tax declarations, encompassing any investments made in local enterprises. I would like to draw attention to this matter, as it is crucial to uphold coherence in tax documentation. For instance, in the situation where you discover that one of your investment partners involved in a real estate trust intends to evade reporting their income, it becomes imperative to ensure their compliance in fulfilling their tax obligations in order to avoid any potential consequences such as a tax audit for both you and your partner. The aforementioned also holds true when considering investments in restaurants or local enterprises; it is imperative to verify the consistency of tax returns and ensure all individuals participating in the investment are meticulously complying with tax reporting requirements.

Inform Yourself

After choosing a benchmark that signifies the realization of your goal to attain wealth, it becomes necessary to embark on the path of self-enrichment to acquire the knowledge and skills essential for its attainment.

The enhancement of financial literacy is an ongoing endeavor that demands perpetual dedication and endeavor on your part. There is an abundance of knowledge to be gained about money, with a constant stream of novel ideas and concepts arising on an annual basis.

Regardless of the extent of your financial knowledge or expertise, it is imperative to take a proactive approach towards your finances rather than neglecting them. The sole means of attaining and retaining wealth lies in equipping oneself with knowledge and diligently employing sound financial management practices (it is observed that the majority of lottery winners deplete their winnings within a few years).

Fortunately, nowadays it is increasingly effortless to augment your comprehension of financial matters and obtain the necessary support to embark on the journey towards financial prosperity.

Numerous online platforms and audio broadcasts related to personal finance offer their expertise on a diverse array of financial topics without any charge. Online platforms such as Reddit and Facebook also host communities dedicated to discussing personal finance matters. Furthermore, Google serves as a highly valuable and reliable source of information.

If you have extensively researched online and remain uncertain about the stability of your financial situation, it would be advisable to contemplate engaging the services of a financial coach to assist in formulating a tailored strategy that aligns with your individual circumstances. Professional mentors have the capacity to assist individuals in overcoming indebtedness, establishing a comprehensive financial plan, or devising a method to accumulate wealth.

Although it is possible to encounter community organizations that offer complimentary financial planning services, such as charitable institutions or your nearby credit union, it is advisable to contemplate engaging a professional financial counselor. Numerous financial advisors exhibit a commendable level of rationality and are capable of guiding you towards initiating your journey until you attain a sufficient

level of confidence to assume full
autonomy.

In the pursuit of self-education, it is
crucial to bear in mind that this
undertaking demands a steadfast
commitment to perpetual growth in
order to achieve your desired outcome.
It is imperative to continuously enhance
one's financial literacy throughout the
course of their lifetime.

Cease Self-Managing Your Personal Affairs.

A common misconception surrounding real estate investment, which often deters individuals from engaging in it, is the belief that investing in real estate requires significant effort and labor. Alternatively, as I have previously suggested, hammer wielding.

As previously stated, I was convinced when I first embarked on my investigation of real estate that the most effective method of investment was to identify motivated traders, negotiate deals, acquire properties, secure tenants, and subsequently lease those tenants. Although I possessed the ability to undertake those activities, I perceived each of them as insurmountable. Upon reflection, I have come to the realization that this is precisely why I initially chose not to pursue a career in real estate—I would have preferred to abstain from engaging in such activities. It was not until I diligently pursued alternative means of investing that I eventually embarked on a journey to become an investor. The aforementioned alternative methods were considerably less involved in nature.

In order to provide you with a contextual understanding of the mechanics behind long-term investing, I will draw a comparison between two distinct methodologies within the realm of property investment. I will first provide a comprehensive explanation of the different approaches, and subsequently, we can engage in a discourse to determine the more optimal choice.

Conventional Real Estate Investment

The conventional approach to investing in rental properties is referred to as investing in an "value enhancement" deal. It is commonly referred to as the 'BRRRR model' in current discourse, wherein 'BRRRR' stands for buy, rehab, rent, refinance, and repeat. You are acquiring a distressed property and subsequently undertaking renovations to enhance the overall value of the property. When executed proficiently, the current valuation of the property, subsequent to your investments for further development, exceeds the initial capital outlay. It entails a comparable concept to property flipping, albeit with the distinction that in these instances, the property is retained and subjected to leasing rather than being sold for a higher value. However, by retaining ownership, the value you have contributed now becomes integrated equity in the property, constituting a vital component of your overall potential gains. In the framework of this investment property acquisition strategy, the process would unfold as follows:

1. Find a property. You have the ability to locate properties through a multitude of sources. You are welcome to collaborate with wholesalers, diligently search the Multiple Listing Service to

secure a favorable deal as soon as it becomes available, and make inquiries with property owners to assess their interest in selling... Sometimes, it is necessary to employ creativity.

2. Negotiate the arrangement. Once you have examined the desired arrangement, it is imperative to collaborate with a professional or distributor to ensure that all necessary procedures are completed in order to finalize the agreement.

3. Close the arrangement. This necessitates collaborating with your financial institution, conducting a thorough property assessment, and fulfilling a diverse array of appropriate due diligence tasks.

4. Rehab the property. Begin swinging those hammers!

5. Find occupants. You are required to engage in advertising efforts to attract prospective tenants, subsequently initiate the application process upon receiving interest, and ultimately

execute a lease agreement with them, facilitating their smooth transition into the property.

6. Landlord the property. You are actively attending to support (and demonstration) calls, and either resolving issues independently or deploying skilled personnel to address them. You maintain awareness of the prevailing laws governing investment properties in your area and ensure strict adherence to them. Ultimately, you will be responsible for both the resident and the physical premises. Furthermore, in the event that a resident requires relocation, you are responsible for overseeing that procedure.

End-to-end Rental Property Investment Solutions

The concept that underlies a turnkey investment property, as well as its etymology, is centered around the notion that all that is required of an investor is to symbolically insert the key into the entrance, rotate it, and immediately begin generating income. This would imply that the property is well-prepared for lease, indicating that no further renovations are needed, and the occupants are currently secured and paying rent.

Whilst the term 'turnkey' (also spelled 'turn key' and 'turn-key') does indeed refer to the condition of a property, on occasion, individuals who are discussing investments in turnkey properties are actually procuring these properties from authentic turnkey enterprises. These entities, commonly referred to as turnkey suppliers, proactively seek out distressed properties, acquire them, and undertake their restoration.

Assign occupants to these spaces, and establish property management to oversee the properties upon acquisition by the investor. Essentially, they are carrying out all of the work pertaining to enhancing reputation as mentioned earlier. This suggests that the work in question is not solely performed by me, the individual providing financial support. Assuming all conditions are equal, the pattern of my contribution cycle would resemble the following:

1. Choose a property that I find appealing. The turnkey suppliers furnish me with a comprehensive inventory of available assets, from which I make my selection.

2. Sign the agreement. Please affix your signature and return it to the sender.

3. Do due industriousness. The primary progression is to verify the accuracy of the property's advertising. It is imperative to conduct a thorough property investigation and verify all numerical data.

4. Close on the property. Sign the end documents.

5. Manage the property supervisor. This matter is inconsequential—it simply pertains to ensuring that the property is progressing according to expectations. The utmost conceivable outcome regarding effort would be the potential

necessity to terminate the property manager if he or she fails to fulfill their duties, and subsequently hire a replacement. Nonetheless, I have no intention of personally attending to any maintenance tasks or engaging in direct communication with any tenants.

Can you perceive a significant disparity in job roles between the two circumstances? The length of the rundowns may appear comparable; however, there exists significant variation in the extent of each method employed between the two approaches. The degree of obligation associated with the conventional approach is considerably lesser in comparison to that of the turnkey technique.

Based on those depictions, you might be inquiring as to the rationale behind individuals choosing to undertake arduous tasks when they could simply excel beyond everyone's expectations and delegate the completion of all their work to others.

It all boils down to the figures.

Methods For Establishing An Investment Chronology

Developing an investment timeline revolves around effectively navigating and regulating one's expectations. When one possesses acute awareness of the latent opportunities within the market, it becomes effortless to become entangled in the fervor. Numerous investors partake in the exercise of unrealistic optimism. They have a faith in their ability to secure a substantial agreement that will effectively resolve all of their issues.

This is an occurrence typically reserved for cinematic portrayals.

Although it is feasible to achieve exceptional results, accomplishing such feats necessitates considerable time and diligent investigation. If you possess the ability to identify such advantageous opportunities, you are likely positioned to achieve substantial gains. Alternatively, otherwise, you may discover yourself in pursuit of the hard-to-find significant opportunity."

Managing Expectations

A crucial aspect of effectively managing expectations is maintaining a sense of realism. By using the term "realistic," we are referring to the recognition that constructing a successful strategy requires a significant amount of time. Hence, it is imperative to exercise patience during the initial stages. As an illustration, a reasonable expectation would be to earn a few hundred dollars within the initial month of engaging in trading. While it may fall short of covering all your expenses, it would nonetheless be a most fortuitous boon.

It is nearly impracticable to precisely specify the monetary amount that one could potentially earn during the initial weeks of engaging in trading activities. The potential profit range varies based on your chosen approach and initial investment, spanning from a few hundred dollars to several thousand. Nevertheless, it is crucial to bear in mind that the majority of investors experience initial financial losses. By adhering to their predetermined strategy, they successfully reverse the situation and regain the lost progress.

Taking this into consideration, it can be reasonably inferred that you will generate sufficient income initially to supplement your monthly earnings. Should you commence with an initial investment amount, such as a few hundred dollars, there exists the potential to amass a sum in excess of $100.

Presented herein is a rational method for ascertaining potential earnings, taking into consideration your initial capital. On an annual basis, the typical returns observed in the market are within the range of 5% to 10%. If we analyze it, that amounts to approximately 1% to 2% per month. That may appear to be an insignificant quantity. However, when you extrapolate this across the spectrum of transactions and investment capital, there exists a considerable potential for generating a substantial sum of money. Subsequently, we will delve into the methodologies you can employ to optimize your profits.

The attainment of absolute financial autonomy varies among investors at various stages of their lives. The straightforward response to this matter is as follows: the more minimalist your lifestyle, the earlier you can achieve financial autonomy. Therefore, should your monthly financial requirements amount to a mere $1,500, it is highly plausible that you may attain this goal within a span of a few years, if not significantly sooner. On the contrary, if your living expenses require a monthly budget of $5,000, it is plausible that achieving that monetary goal may entail a significant time frame of multiple years. Ultimately, it ultimately comes down to your overarching way of life.

Investment In Crypto

Is your interest solely driven by the current hype surrounding the bitcoin phenomenon? Are there any valid justifications for allocating investments specifically towards one or more digital tokens?

A significant proportion of individuals express a keen interest in embarking upon a career in the bitcoin industry due to the following motivations:

"Cryptocurrency fervor" is a prevalent phenomenon.

Desire to swiftly and effortlessly generate income.

Maintain confidence in their extensive knowledge.

Embarking on a new project would serve as a welcomed respite following a protracted phase of dedication.

Based on the aforementioned justifications, it is inadvisable to engage in a cryptocurrency investment. Prior to engaging in cryptocurrency investments, it is imperative to conduct thorough research.

2.1 What is the Methodology for Investing in Cryptocurrencies?

The subsequent recommendations will aid you in ascertaining how to initiate your cryptocurrency journey:

Acquire knowledge about the sector

It is imperative, particularly for individuals new to digital currencies, to acquire a comprehensive understanding of the functioning of the digital currency realm prior to making any investments. Please allocate sufficient time to acquaint yourself with the different currencies at your disposal. Given the multitude of currencies and tokens available, it is imperative to extend one's assessment beyond the widely recognized denominations such as Bitcoin, Ripple, and Ether.

Gaining knowledge about blockchain technology is equally imperative to comprehending the functioning of this integral aspect within the bitcoin industry.

Comprehending certain aspects of blockchain technology might pose challenges if one lacks a background in computer science or coding. There exists a wide array of introductory manuals pertaining to the subject of blockchain technology.

After you have made the decision to invest in a cryptocurrency, or perhaps multiple cryptocurrencies, it is imperative to examine the manner in which those tokens utilize blockchain technology and assess if they offer any distinctive attributes that differentiate them from their competitors. You will enhance your ability to assess the viability of a potential investment opportunity by developing a comprehensive understanding of cryptocurrencies and blockchain technology.

Participate in an online community dedicated to cryptocurrency enthusiasts.

Due to the current prominence of digital currency, developments occur at a rapid pace. This can be attributed, at least in part, to the active and ongoing discourse within the community of digital currency investors and enthusiasts.

Enroll in our group to remain informed about the current developments in the bitcoin sector. Despite the fact that Reddit has emerged as a prominent hub for enthusiasts of digital currency, there exist a plethora of alternative online forums where ongoing discussions take place.

Please peruse whitepapers pertaining to cryptocurrency.

The attributes of digital currency hold greater significance, as opposed to mere speculation. Please dedicate some time and effort to explore the official document outlining the details and objectives of the project that you are considering investing in. This feature is essential for every cryptocurrency project and should be easily accessible to the general public.

The white paper is intended to provide comprehensive information regarding the project's authors' intentions, encompassing a timeline, an all-encompassing project overview, as well as specific details. Read it carefully. White papers that are devoid of empirical evidence and precise details concerning the project are frequently perceived in an unfavorable light. Development teams utilize a white paper as a means to comprehensively outline the goals and objectives of their project. Should any portion of the white paper appear insufficient or misleading, this could potentially signify underlying issues within the project.

It all depends on the timing.

Through your extensive examination, you have likely acquired an understanding of the cryptocurrency industry, and consequently, you have made informed choices regarding one or more investment opportunities. The subsequent step involves ascertaining the optimal moment for investment. The realm of digital currencies experiences rapid evolution and is widely recognized for its inherent volatility.

Firstly, investing in the emerging currency prior to its meteoric rise in popularity and worth has the potential to compel other investors to follow suit. In actuality, conducting sector surveillance prior to taking action will enhance your prospects of achieving success. Cryptocurrencies exhibit distinctive patterns in terms of their pricing dynamics. Bitcoin frequently leads the way within the realm of virtual currencies, setting the precedent for others that subsequently emulate its trajectory. Certainly, the cryptocurrency realm may experience widespread repercussions when confronted with instances of exchange breach, price manipulation, or fraudulent activities. Therefore, it is imperative to diligently monitor the prevailing developments.

In conclusion, it is important to note that cryptocurrencies should be regarded as a financially precarious investment option. Numerous additional investors have contributed funds to the realm of digital tokens solely to witness its dissipation alongside the sudden emergence of bitcoin billionaires. Engaging in investment in this sector involves assuming a certain level of risk. Enhancing the likelihood of achievement can be achieved through the completion of your study prior to engaging in any investment.

Investing Principles

The cornerstone of achieving success in investments lies in adhering to a well-established set of principles that have proven effective over time. The principles elucidated in this chapter will facilitate your discernment of potential opportunities and expeditiously guide you in dismissing those that are incongruous with your objectives. It is imperative to eliminate unfavorable prospects, as there exist a multitude of companies and circumstances that warrant consideration for investment purposes.

Prominent investors effectively channel their attention towards domains where they possess a distinct advantage, and adhering to these principles will facilitate seamless execution of this approach. Without any additional delay or hesitation, let us proceed to discuss the initial principle.

Principle One

Consider the hypothetical situation where you are an adept high school football player. You ultimately secure a scholarship to participate in collegiate football and successfully distinguish yourself at that competitive echelon. You are selected by the NFL and are anticipated to achieve considerable success within the league. Nevertheless, shortly after being selected, you make the choice to pursue a baseball career instead, despite not having engaged in formal training for the sport since your middle school years.

This behavior is not commonly observed among individuals. Indeed, what would compel an individual to engage in such an idiocy? What rationale would lead an individual to dedicate considerable effort towards honing their skills in a specific domain, only to deliberately overlook their competency and engage in an alternative pursuit? It is advisable to focus on tasks and endeavors in which you possess a competitive advantage.

Each individual possesses a level of proficiency in specific domains. Whether attributed to innate talent, fortunate circumstances, or relentless determination, each of us possesses inherent aptitudes. By diverting our attention and exerting high levels of effort, we can cultivate that expertise to attain a genuinely eminent status on a global scale. Please take note that these skills encompass both cognitive and physical abilities.

Certain individuals possess inherent inclinations towards creativity, while others demonstrate a greater inclination towards analytical thinking. Other individuals possess inherent physical talents that contribute to their exceptional athleticism, and so forth. In summary, every individual possesses inherent aptitude in a particular area, and the optimal path to achievement lies in selecting pursuits that align with those aptitudes. It is illogical to expect an athlete to perform in an office cubicle setting.

What is the relevance of all this information in relation to investment? To put it succinctly, it implies the necessity of adhering to games or circumstances in which one possesses a distinct advantage. It is possible that you have accumulated substantial professional experience in a particular industry or have devoted substantial effort to cultivate extensive knowledge in it. Irrespective of the limited extent of your experience, you possess insights in specific domains that others may lack, even if you have yet to acknowledge them (Graham, 1998).

By adhering to these concepts and scenarios that you perceive as comprehensible, the attainment of profitable investments becomes significantly facilitated and likely. It is essential to acknowledge the significance of the term probable, given that all aspects within the market revolve around probabilities. It is imperative to remember that guarantees are non-existent, and one can only depend on the likelihood of outcomes.

Optimal outcomes can be achieved by strategically selecting circumstances that provide a favorable advantage. Therefore, it is imperative that you engage in ventures that are within your comprehension and can be assessed with astuteness. By doing so, you will inherently enhance your likelihood of achieving favorable outcomes. Similar to the comparative advantage enjoyed by an individual who has devoted their entire existence to honing their skills in football, as opposed to an individual who recently picked up the sport, it is crucial that you direct your attention towards circumstances that provide you with a strategic advantage.

Your initial response may perhaps lead you to believe that you possess limited knowledge on various subjects. This assertion is unfounded, as it is a widely acknowledged fact that individuals possess knowledge in varying degrees across diverse subjects. It is not imperative for one to possess expertise at this moment, as competence can invariably be developed in a given field. Regarding investments, this entails enhancing your expertise in assessing a specific industry or sector.

A comprehensive comprehension is essential for assessing the economic dynamics of a sector and the qualitative attributes of a business. Ideally, there will be someone providing an explanation of these matters to you. Regrettably, the industry's chief executive officers will not allocate their time to provide explanations to you. Nevertheless, there exists a suitable alternative for this: the 10-K annual reports that publicly traded corporations submit to the Securities and Exchange Commission (SEC).

These documents encompass comprehensive elucidation of the enterprise's operational domain and the obstacles it confronts. In addition, comprehensive analysis of managerial deliberations regarding business circumstances and explanations of their intended strategies can be found.

It may appear overly simplistic to state that the sole requirement is the diligent examination of 10-K reports, yet this is the methodology employed by the esteemed billionaire investor, Warren Buffett. Granted, his accomplishments are not solely attributable to the mere act of perusing a multitude of annual reports. However, delving into and evaluating a corporation's financial statements through the utilization of the 10-K form serves as the bedrock upon which his achievements are built.

Numerous investors opt to disregard 10-Ks due to the required effort and concentration entailed in their analysis. The typical 10-K report spans more than 100 pages, which can appear daunting. The initial reports you peruse may initially cause a sense of bewilderment, but as you become more accustomed to the task, it will gradually become less daunting (Palmer, 2019).

While the act of perusing 10-K reports represents a commendable practice, it is imperative that you initiate a process of exploring prospects within sectors and industries that are within your realm of comprehension. As an illustration, if you believe you can comprehend the intricacies of a fast-food chain's operations, it would be illogical to consider investing in an investment bank. It would be more advisable to explore McDonald's business rather than that of Goldman Sachs.

Even if you possess incomplete comprehension of a business, initiate by introspecting about the aspects where your understanding surpasses that of others. Is your comprehension regarding a fast-food chain superior to that of a financial institution? Do you believe you possess a greater aptitude for comprehending the intricacies of banks as opposed to airlines? Commence the investigation from a designated point and analyze the annual reports (10-Ks) of the companies operating within that industry. If you encounter a level of complexity that you find challenging, it may be advisable to transition to an alternative task or endeavor.

There is an abundant number of businesses in the United States that present exceptional prospects. Commence at a certain point and in due course, you will discover those that are of exceptional quality. Consistently adhere to your areas of expertise and refrain from deviating from them. The opportunities of which you are uninformed are not regarded as "misses," but rather circumstances in which you lacked any advantage, hence lacking any justification for your involvement.

The Value Of A Stock

Introduction

Envision a box containing twelve doughnuts placed before you. What would be the price you are willing to offer for a single donut? If all the donuts in the box are identical, does one hold a higher value than the others? Imagine a hypothetical scenario in which the global supply of sugar faces a severe shortage, resulting in the depletion of all remaining donuts worldwide, and rendering their production impossible for the ensuing year. Does the limited availability elevate the inherent worth of the commodity? If one were to consume an entire box of donuts and subsequently find oneself unable to consume any more, would the price one would be willing to pay for an additional donut decrease?

The assortment of twelve doughnuts serves as a representation of a company. When the organization is dissected, everyone is afforded the chance to acquire a stake in the donuts, or a portion of the company. However, individuals may encounter significant disparity in pricing for identical pastries. If you desire to optimize the value of a box of donuts, what could be the most effective method? One approach is to persuade individuals that these are the most delectable donuts globally and that their availability is only temporary. Concisely summarizing, this is the functioning mechanism of the market. The stock market is comprised of individuals who experience varying levels of enthusiasm or dissatisfaction based on their emotional state. What is evident is that periodically the market experiences volatility.

Please take into account the viewing of the subsequent video presentation in which esteemed investor Warren Buffett provides insights on his response to the query, "How do you react when the market experiences a decline?" It is worth examining how Warren Buffett employs sound judgment in identifying opportunities during instances when assets are priced favorably. Do you concur with his perspective?

What are the factors contributing to significant volatility in stock prices?

Access a reputable financial newspaper such as the Wall Street Journal. Navigate to the stock quote section, select any company in a random fashion, and analyze the historical high and low stock prices over the preceding year. Alternatively, users may visit the Yahoo Finance website to proceed. Now, let us examine the information at hand. We have GM. They engage in the manufacturing of automobiles and commercial vehicles. During the preceding 52-week period, the shares of the company experienced a trading range between $28 per share and $39 per share. The number of shares outstanding for GM amounts to 1.6

billion (bn), implying that the market value of GM ranged between $45bn and $62bn. That constitutes a disparity of $17 billion in monetary worth. The automobile industry experiences minimal changes over time. You have an annual sales increase of approximately 5% for vehicles. The Chevrolet Silverado is a model specifically known as the Chevy Silverado. However, it is not currently engaged in the pursuit of either replacing gasoline with water as fuel or developing the technology to facilitate lunar travel. The business remains fundamentally unchanged this year in comparison to the previous year. How is it possible for the value to experience a $17 billion fluctuation? Furthermore, why is this phenomenon occurring universally across every company in the stock market?

Did last year experience notable fluctuations in prices? Is there any undisclosed knowledge or information that the market possesses, which remains unknown to us? No.

So, what's the explanation? The market is exhibiting significant volatility and erratic behavior.

MR. MARKET

Allow me to recount a narrative. This is an anecdote shared by renowned investor Benjamin Graham. It pertains to an individual who is a business associate of yours, specifically Mr. Market. Envisage a situation where you and another individual jointly possess a business. Currently, Mr. Market exhibits commendable qualities; however, he is prone to erratic fluctuations in his disposition. At the break of dawn, he awakens to find the azure heavens adorning the firmament, and experiences an overwhelming sense of contentment and vitality coursing through his being. Therefore, he proposes an offer to acquire your ownership stake in the business at a substantially higher value than its current worth. The following day, he awakens to rain shower outside.

Experiencing profound despair and exclaiming apocalyptically about the impending doom of the world. He proposes to sell the entire stock he owns in the company to you at a discounted price of fifty percent of the original amount you paid for it. You accept the offer. The following day, Mr. Market presents a price that is neither unusually high nor unusually low, prompting you to refrain from taking any action. The business's intrinsic value remained relatively stable over time; what fluctuated were the unpredictable shifts in Mr. Market's sentiments. In summary, Mr. Market exhibits volatile mood swings.

Does this imply that we should refrain from making investments in the stock market owing to these volatile fluctuations in the short term? Contrarily! The mere fact that occasional deals are extended to us should evoke a profound sense of excitement. Our objective is twofold: firstly, to ascertain the valuation of the company, and secondly, to seize opportune moments when Mr. Market experiences a downturn, allowing us to acquire it at a significant markdown. According to Benjamin Graham, this practice can be described as creating a "safety cushion." In essence, it can be likened to acquiring dollar bills for a mere fifty cents.

Ok, you're thinking. This is commendable and satisfactory. Exercise patience until the market experiences volatility and acquire assets at a price below their intrinsic value. Nonetheless, a single predicament persists: How can we ascertain with certainty the extent to which we can comprehend the true worth of a corporation? How can we attain assurance regarding the accuracy of our forecasts (commonly referred to as mere conjectures) and their alignment with reality? Are there not numerous intelligent individuals and computer programs eagerly anticipating the opportunity to acquire a favorable deal as soon as it presents itself?

Contrary to popular belief, the number is actually lower than one might anticipate.

POINT FOR REFLECTION: "

1. Contemplate an item or purchase for which you managed to obtain a highly advantageous arrangement in the past. How did you successfully secure such a advantageous transaction? How does this bear resemblance to the stock market?

Buying Calls

B

Purchasing call options represents a more advanced methodology of instruction compared to engaging in the practice of selling covered calls. However, the intricacy of the subject matter warrants our exploration.

The Actual Purchases Being Made

It is important to keep in mind that a single option contract represents a quantity of 100 shares. Therefore, it is necessary to have the capacity to procure 100 shares of the stock in order to exercise the privilege of purchase.

Additionally, it is important to bear in mind that an options contract possesses a predetermined expiration date. In the event that the stock price does not surpass the strike price within the prescribed time frame, you will unfortunately be at a disadvantage, resulting in the loss of the entirety of the funds you allocated towards the premium. From a comparative standpoint, the additional cost will be minimal. Therefore, if you exercise caution and refrain from initially purchasing a large quantity of options contracts, the financial loss incurred is likely to be insignificant.

Available alternatives for achieving your purchasing objectives through options contracts

The objective in acquiring options contracts is to secure a stock at a price that is below its existing market valuation. To put it differently, your objective is for the stock price to surpass the strike price by a noteworthy margin, facilitating substantial cost savings when purchasing the stock. When conducting an assessment of your alternatives, it is crucial to factor in the supplementary expenses comprised of the premium paid and associated commissions. In certain instances, the magnitude of commissions can be significant. Hence, it is imperative to be well-informed regarding these charges in advance. This knowledge will enable you to select an optimal strike price and appropriately exercise your options in due course.

You act as a trader rather than an investor.

You might have developed a cognitive inclination towards contemplating investment strategies. A prospective investor aims to construct a well-balanced investment portfolio over an extended duration, with the conviction that it will appreciate in value over the long term. A trader functions within the same realm, although their objectives may diverge. You prioritize immediate financial gains rather than long-term investments. You will refrain from retaining ownership of this stock. If you were inclined to possess the stock, you would acquire it at the present lower price being offered. The objective is to acquire the stocks at the strike price after a substantial increase in their value, promptly selling them in order to realize the resulting gains.

Let's take an example. Assuming that the current market price of XYZ Corporation stands at $30 per share. Individuals anticipate an upward trajectory for the stock, with a certain segment expressing notable optimism regarding its immediate future. If you are an investor, your objective is to acquire the stock at the most optimal price and subsequently retain it for the long haul. If one employs techniques such as dollar-cost averaging, they may acquire a few shares each month without placing significant emphasis on the specific price at which they make the purchase. In any event, as an investor, you will strictly acquire the shares at a price of $30.

As a trader, you are seeking to capitalize on the price fluctuations of XYZ in the forthcoming months. You will proceed to purchase an options contract, given that its premium is $0.90 and the strike price is set at $35. The cost of the 100 shares amounts to $90.

Subsequently, the stock price experiences a rapid increase, reaching a value of $45. Given that the strike price has been surpassed, you have the opportunity to exercise your option to acquire the shares at the predetermined strike price. These items are available for purchase at a unit price of $35, resulting in a cumulative expenditure of $3,500. However, it is important to note that you do not hold a long-term investment perspective. You will promptly dispose of the shares. You vend the stocks for a sum of $4,500, thereby generating a profit of $1,000. Upon careful evaluation of the premium you have paid, it has been determined that your profit amounts to $910. After taking into account commissions, the price will decrease slightly; however, the main concept remains unchanged. The objective of purchasing call options is to swiftly generate returns on stocks that you anticipate will experience a rapid increase in value.

It is challenging to determine the optimal timing for purchasing call options. Naturally, it would be ill-advised to undertake such actions during a significant economic downturn. The most advantageous period is when the market is experiencing a bullish trend or when a particular company is anticipated to make a significant breakthrough, leading to a sudden surge in its market valuation. Another opportune moment to consider is during an economic recession, as it signifies the conclusion of the downturn phase.

www.ingramcontent.com/pod-product-compliance
Lightning Source LLC
Chambersburg PA
CBHW061021220326
41597CB00016BB/1934